A L
RUBBISH

THE SCIENCE OF WASTE DISPOSAL

BY
LESLEY
NEWSON

ILLUSTRATED BY
MIKE GORDON

SIMON & SCHUSTER

LONDON • SYDNEY • NEW YORK • TOKYO • SINGAPORE • TORONTO

First published in Great Britain in 1990
by Simon & Schuster Young Books

Simon & Schuster Young Books
Simon & Schuster International Group
Wolsey House, Wolsey Road
Hemel Hempstead HP2 4SS

British Library Cataloguing in Publication Data
Newson, Lesley
A Load of Rubbish.
1. Refuse
1. Title
628.44
ISBN 0-7500-0273-5

Printed in Great Britain by BPCC Wheatons Ltd, Exeter

Contents

A Very Big Load

How much rubbish do you think you created in the last year? How many sweet wrappers, crisp bags, yoghurt pots and apple cores did you toss in the bin?

The rubbish you make in a week would probably cover your bedroom floor. After a few months it could be a metre deep. In a year, you make a pile of rubbish that weighs about ten times as much as you. Everyone else also makes a lot of rubbish, about one-third of a tonne per person every year in Britain. It all adds up to an extremely large load of rubbish.

All this rubbish doesn't just take up space and look untidy. It's dangerous. If we allowed rubbish to pile up around our homes, mice, rats and other animals would soon come to eat the food we didn't want. Flies would lay their eggs in it too. These would hatch into maggots and then mature into more flies. And, as rubbish rots it not only becomes smelly, but also poisonous. You can see for yourself how this happens. All you need is a number of jars with screw top lids. Seal samples of food such as bread, fruit, vegetables or meat inside each jar and leave them in a warm, light place. Look at them after a week. What can you see? Be careful to dispose of the samples carefully, and don't sniff the jars or taste their contents. Don't forget to wash your hands afterwards.

Do you know where rubbish goes when it's taken away from your home? Wherever it's taken is bound to be near other people's homes. And many of them are probably complaining about it. It is also bound to be near the homes of millions of animals, plants and micro-organisms. They can't fight to protect their habitat. But many people believe that we should fight for them, and pay as much attention to protecting the natural world as we do to protecting people and property.

So what is done to prevent your rubbish causing harm? Should we do more? Do we need to make so much rubbish?

Perhaps the first thing to think about is that Nature has found solutions to the problem of waste which have worked for a very long time. It is only relatively recently that the amount and type of rubbish we create has become a problem.

How Nature Does It

To really understand the problem of rubbish and some of the ways it might be solved, it's best to go back to the beginning of life on Earth, 3,500 million years ago.

Making rubbish is part of life, and not just of human life. To stay alive, all living things have to take in substances such as air, water and nutrients from the world around them – from their 'environment'. As they use these substances they release other substances back into the environment as waste. When they die, their dead bodies are no longer needed and therefore become rubbish.

Life has been going on for millions of years, and countless trillions of creatures have lived and died. Fossils provide us with the evidence that these creatures did live, but the Earth isn't polluted with their waste. It all seems to have disappeared.

You can see this for yourself by burying a small scrap of meat in your garden, just below the surface of the soil. Carefully mark the spot, then leave it for a few weeks. Wearing gloves you can then sift through the soil to see what is left.

Waste disappears because it is 'recycled'. In Nature, the waste produced by one living creature is useful to another. Flies and many other insects lay their eggs in fallen fruit, dung and dead bodies of larger creatures which act as food when the maggots hatch. Ants, termites, woodlice and many other tiny animals feed on plant waste. But most of Nature's recycling work is done by even smaller creatures, microscopically small organisms like bacteria and fungi. There are millions of different types and between them they can eat almost anything.

The work of micro-organisms can be seen all around us. They make milk sour, bread mouldy and wood rotten. The awful smell of rubbish that is a few days old is caused by the work of micro-organisms, usually bacteria. As they digest our waste, they produce waste chemicals of their own. These often taste and smell bad and they can be poisonous. But this rather nasty waste is eaten by other bacteria and their waste is food for other bacteria, and so on. In time, bacteria can completely digest much of our waste so that it is no longer smelly or dangerous.

In the natural world, the recycling system usually works very well. For example, a squirrel eating acorns in an oak wood leaves behind the acorn shells and its own body wastes, faeces and urine. Once micro-organisms have completely digested this waste, the simple chemicals that remain become part of the soil or the air. Oak trees need to take in these chemicals so they can grow and produce more acorns.

Sometimes though, Nature's recycling system cannot complete the job. A small amount of the waste made by living creatures has been left behind.

For Nature to do a complete recycling job, the waste-eating micro-organisms need plenty of air. Occasionally the bodies of sea creatures became trapped in mud on the sea bed. Sometimes trees and other plants fell into a bog. Under these conditions, there was not enough air to allow micro-organisms to break down the waste completely into the simple chemicals that plants can use. Instead it was changed into something else. There are bacteria that can digest waste in an airless environment, but they turn the waste into some quite complicated and often rather dangerous chemicals.

All over the Earth there are pockets of these unrecycled wastes buried underground. They are the oil, gas and coal deposits that we use as fuel.

Waste Becomes a Problem

When the first humans appeared on earth about two and a half million years ago, Nature dealt with their rubbish in the same way as it did with the waste of other animals. After all, the early humans lived in pretty much the same way as animals. They hunted and gathered their food as they needed it, ate it as they found it and left their waste on the ground. They had no permanent homes so if their rubbish got too smelly, they just moved away.

However, about 10,000 years ago, people learnt that they could cultivate plants, rather than just harvesting the wild plants they found. They no longer needed to be nomadic hunter-gatherers. They became farmers. This was the beginning of what we call civilization. But it was also the beginning of serious rubbish problems.

Farming gave people more reliable supplies of food. This meant they could raise larger families, so the population began to grow. Settling down also meant they could build permanent and more comfortable houses.

But now, for the first time, human beings had to deal with the problem of rubbish. They could no longer just move out once the rubbish pile got too big. But they had to do something! At first, the rubbish was probably just taken out of the village to the surrounding countryside. Farmers allowed it to rot for a while and then mixed it in with the soil. This made the soil more fertile by adding nutrients that crops needed to grow.

Some kinds of rubbish could also be fed to animals. In countries such as Britain, many families kept a pig. It fed on their rubbish, getting rid of much of it, and could be eaten once it had grown fat.

Families also used to burn rubbish on their cooking fires, although they then had the problem of getting rid of the ashes. These took up less space than unburned rubbish and didn't smell or attract flies, but they were also less useful. Animals couldn't eat them and farmers didn't want them on their land.

Before long, people who owned land in or near a town realized they could make money by disposing of other people's rubbish. They dug big holes called middens. Since people were charged by the amount of rubbish they threw in the midden, everyone was careful to throw away as little as possible.

None of these ways of disposing of rubbish was ideal. Using rotted down rubbish to improve the soil worked well for small farming villages, but as towns got larger and more crowded, carting rubbish all the way out to the fields became difficult. Burning rubbish also caused more problems as towns grew larger. The smoke in the air mixed with the smell of rotting rubbish and animal dung, making town life unpleasant and unhealthy.

Huge numbers of rats and flies lived in the towns eating rubbish and anything else they could find. Many rats grew large enough to kill young babies, and they would bite anyone. They spread diseases by carrying bacteria on their bodies, and also by providing a home in their fur for fleas that bit humans and infected them with bubonic plague. In one plague epidemic in 1349, one-third of the population of England died.

Pigs often caught diseases from eating rubbish and sometimes these were passed on to people who ate the meat. Jews and Moslems were forbidden to eat this 'unclean' meat, while others were warned to cook it thoroughly.

The Rubbish Explosion

About 200 years ago, people discovered that coal could be used to power machinery. Machines were invented that could do many types of work that had always been done by hand or with the help of animals.

This made many goods quicker and cheaper to produce. People who lived 200 years ago could afford to own very little. Most only had one or two sets of clothing, for example, and these were often old clothes already well worn by someone who was richer, older, or who had died. Even something like paper, which litters our streets today, was precious 200 years ago. And, since most people couldn't read, they wouldn't buy newspapers or books even if they could afford them.

Today people often complain about the 'rising cost of living', but we have far more possessions than people did 200 years ago. Unfortunately, owning more things has meant making more rubbish, as everything we buy eventually gets broken or worn out and has to be thrown away.

At first, many of the factory-made things were recycled. Old clothing and rags were sold to factories and used as raw material for the manufacture of new cloth or paper. Even old metal saucepans were melted down and turned into new ones.

But things kept on getting cheaper, and in time, some things became so cheap, people could afford to use them once and throw them away. The first throwaway items were made of paper. Then, as the price of making glass and some metals came down, these became disposable too. Food was sold in jars and tins which could be thrown in the bin once they'd been emptied. Re-using them just seemed more trouble than it was worth. In time, almost everyone began to believe that an empty jar or tin was just rubbish.

Then came the discoveries that changed the nature of the rubbish problem again. Scientists found that the chemicals in fossil fuels – coal, gas and oil could be made into completely new materials.

PLASTICS

One of the new materials was plastic. Plastic is durable and it comes in many different forms. Think of all the objects and packages around your home that are made of plastic and think about how much plastic you throw away each week.

Other materials made from oil or coal can be made into the fibres of new fabrics for clothing. Before the invention of these 'synthetic' fibres, cloth could only be made of the natural fibres – cotton, linen, wool and silk. Look at the labels of your clothes to see how many of them contain only natural fibres and how many are made of other materials. Synthetic fabrics have helped make clothing so cheap that many people can afford to buy a whole new set of clothes every year. The old ones sometimes just get thrown away.

Fertilizer made from fossil fuels makes it possible to grow food in far greater quantities. Although people in many parts of the world don't have enough to eat, food is now so plentiful in some countries that much of it is wasted. How much food is in your bin just because someone didn't want to eat it?

Over the last 200 years, people became so good at making things cheaply, they believed they could afford to be wasteful. The result is a very large load of rubbish. The rubbish made by a person living 200 years ago was mostly in the form of ash, and a week's worth of rubbish, about a kilogram, would barely have covered the bottom of a modern rubbish bin. Today each person living in Europe makes between eight and nine kilograms of rubbish each week. Americans and Canadians produce even more, closer to 11 kilograms per week.

Another problem is that there now are far more people on Earth making rubbish. Two hundred years ago, the Earth's population was less than a thousand million. Today there are six or seven times as many people and our numbers are increasing faster than ever.

Some people blame modern science and technology for our rubbish problems. Certainly without scientific advances, we wouldn't have the same problems, because life would be different. But we would still have problems of creating and disposing of rubbish to add to those of more disease, extreme poverty, and a less interesting life.

Someone Else's Problem

As the rubbish problem grew, some people realized that it could provide some well-paid jobs. In exchange for money, they collected and disposed of other people's rubbish. Each day, people put their rubbish in a bin and, since the rubbish was mostly made up of ashes which were very dusty, they called it the 'dustbin'. Every week or so, a 'dust cart' would come around and empty the bin. The rubbish was then someone else's problem.

When these services first started, many were unreliable, and some just carted the rubbish out of town and dumped it somewhere in the country when no-one was looking. Finally, most countries began to realize that rubbish was a serious problem and governments passed laws about how rubbish should be handled. Local government officials became responsible for making sure that the rubbish was collected regularly from every home. This was usually paid for from taxes or rates.

At first, this seemed to be an ideal solution to the rubbish problem, but it was probably one important cause of the problems we have today. Once people no longer had to deal with their own waste, they made no effort to limit the amount of rubbish they created.

The people who had the job of dealing with everyone else's rubbish were expected to dispose of it in a way that would cause no problems. They soon found this to be very difficult. It hasn't got any easier. The rubbish disposal experts of today dispose of waste in the same ways as our ancestors did, by burying it or burning it.

The problem is, not only is there far more rubbish today, but it is a more complicated mixture of things. There is no perfect way of dealing with this mixture because methods that work well for some things, don't work for others.

Landfills – The Modern Middens

Many years ago, people threw their rubbish into huge holes called middens. Today's middens are known as landfill sites.

The basic idea of landfill is to fill a hole or valley with rubbish, or to build a hill of rubbish on some land that isn't wanted for any other purpose. Afterwards the rubbish is covered with a thick layer of earth. Grass and trees are planted, and something useful like a school or shopping centre is built on top. The idea sounds quite simple, but doing it is actually extremely complicated.

Landfill sites can vary in size from one to 300 hectares. (A hectare is approximately the area of a football pitch.) The rubbish can be piled from 10 to 50 metres deep. The largest landfill sites would be able to take the rubbish collected from two million homes for over 100 years before they became full.

The landfill site is divided into sections called 'cells', which are filled in a planned order. Each cell is surrounded by a bank of earth or rubble about three metres high, either dug from the site itself or trucked in from nearby mines, quarries or construction sites which often have a lot of waste earth to get rid of.

As soon as the rubbish lorries empty their loads, bulldozers spread it thinly over the ground. Then compactors drive over the rubbish to flatten and smash it down. The rubbish then takes up less space, is less likely to blow away, and is a firmer ground on which vehicles can drive.

At the end of each day, bulldozers spread a layer of earth or rubble over the rubbish to prevent flies and animals getting into it to feed or breed and to stop smells, flies or wind-blown litter.

The same process is repeated until the cell is filled with rubbish 10 metres deep. Then that cell is covered and work begins on the next. Once a layer of rubbish has been put down all over the site, everything starts again until up to four or five layers have been deposited and the rubbish is covered over with earth.

The Problems of Landfill

Unfortunately, everyone soon learned that covering over rubbish in a landfill was not as good a solution as it had seemed at first.

We now understand the mistake the planners made. They thought of a landfill site as simply land filled with rubbish. It's not. It is an ever-changing mass of trillions of living creatures.

Household rubbish is alive with micro-organisms like bacteria, mould and yeast, all making a meal not only of your food waste, but also of paper, cardboard, wood and some of the cloth we throw away. At first this was not seen as a problem. After all, one living creature making use of the waste of another is Nature's own method of waste disposal. Micro-organisms in the soil eat waste and release the nutrients that plants need to grow.

However, this doesn't happen in a landfill site. To break down the waste completely, micro-organisms need plenty of air. And once the rubbish has been compacted, layered, and buried in a landfill site, micro-organisms living there soon grow very short of air and die. The kinds of bacteria which are able to thrive without air begin to take their place. As these creatures eat they make some extremely unpleasant waste chemicals, which can leak out of the landfill site.

How the waste chemicals make their escape depends on the age and depth of the landfill site. The wastes made by bacteria that live in shallower and newer landfill sites are washed out of the decaying rubbish as rainwater trickles down through the layers. This produces a black and poisonous liquid called 'leachate'. This can overflow from a waterlogged site or seep out of the bottom. If this happens, the leachate can poison wells and water supplies, damaging or killing all the living organisms that use the water.

The bacteria in older and deeper sites make explosive gases that are lighter than air. They rise through the layers of rubbish and earth and can become trapped in buildings and pipes.

Once the problems with landfills were discovered, scientists and engineers had to work fast to find out what goes on in landfills and to design ways of making them safer. They laid pipework into the layers of rubbish to collect the explosive gas so it could be safely burned. In some landfill sites, the burning gas has even been put to use. It warms water to provide central heating for nearby homes or factories. In other sites the water is boiled and the steam used to generate electricity.

No one has been able to find a good use for the leachate but it can become harmless if it seeps from the landfill sites very slowly. If it escapes too quickly, the leachate has to be collected in pipes and then sprinkled slowly onto a field, where it can be broken down by bacteria.

Leachates have to be tested regularly to make sure they don't contain 'heavy metals' like mercury, arsenic, lead and cadmium. These cannot be broken down by bacteria and have to be chemically removed from the leachate. Do you or your family ever throw used batteries into the bin? Did you know that many of them contain some of these highly poisonous heavy metals?

Can you think why today's landfill sites have caused more problems than the middens where our ancestors buried their rubbish? One of the reasons is that our ancestors very rarely buried things that would rot. Their kitchen waste was either fed to animals or burned as fuel.

The work necessary to make landfill sites safer has made disposing of rubbish by landfill much more expensive. And it has become increasingly difficult to find new sites. Filling in old mines and quarries may make them look better, but could be dangerous. Areas which could make suitable landfill sites are often too near homes.

Burning Rubbish

The second main way of disposing of rubbish is by burning it. People have been burning their rubbish as fuel for warmth, light and cooking since pre-historic times. But about 120 years ago, when the number of people and the amount of rubbish they made began to increase to an alarming rate, it became clear that simply putting rubbish on a fire and letting it burn was not a good idea. The smoke from burning rubbish fires was usually thick and smelly, full of particles of unburned rubbish and some poisonous gases.

Even so, until about 30 years ago, many people used to burn a lot of their own rubbish at home in their fireplace or on a bonfire. By then the air in many cities and towns had become so polluted that laws were passed to ban smoky fires. In some towns, large incinerators had been built to burn the rubbish collected from the area, but most of these were also too smoky and had to be closed down.

The burning of rubbish could only continue if engineers were able to design incinerators that would burn the rubbish more cleanly. It was found that far fewer particles of unburned rubbish went up the chimney if the fire was made to burn at temperatures above 600 degrees Celsius, which is three times hotter than the hottest setting of most kitchen ovens. At this temperature the chemicals that give smoke its unpleasant smell were destroyed too but some invisible and odourless fumes remained so the fire had to be made hotter still. At temperatures above 800 degrees, almost all of the chemicals were destroyed.

To be on the safe side, the engineers designed incinerators which would burn at around 1000 degrees. Even hotter incinerators were built to handle particularly dangerous waste chemicals. To keep the temperature high, the fire had to burn continuously and the engineers designed machinery to remove the ash and add rubbish constantly and at exactly the right rate so that a large clump of wet waste wouldn't damp down the flames.

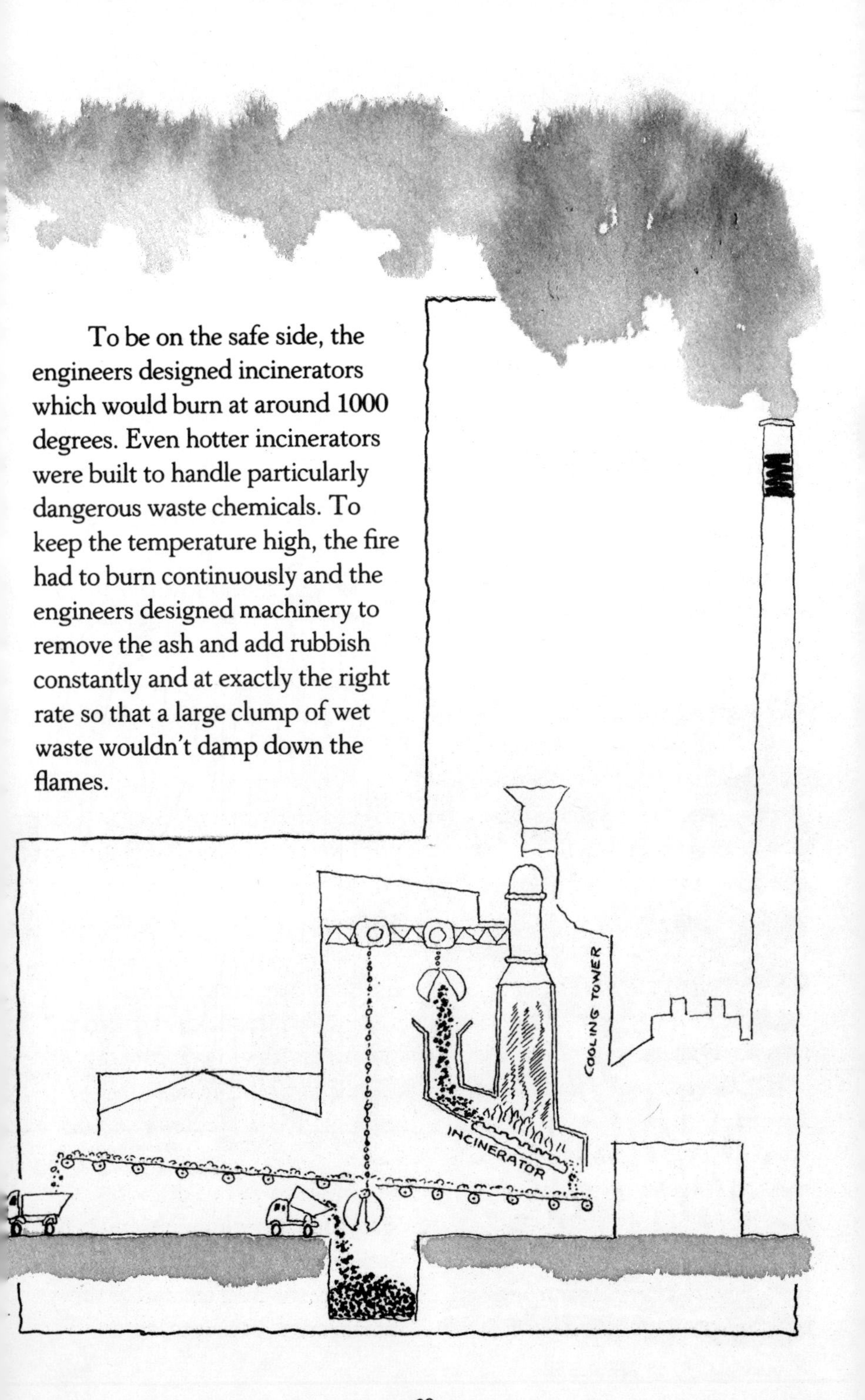

But high temperatures alone cannot prevent incinerators causing air pollution. The hot air that rises from the fire carries tiny particles of ash and dust up the chimney. Any ash in the air causes pollution, but tests showed that this 'fly ash' from incinerators was particularly bad. If rubbish contains poisonous metals, burning it sends those metals up the chimney as part of the fly ash.

To deal with this, two methods of cleaning the smoke were invented. First the hot smoke is cooled with a spray of water. This makes the larger particles of ash drop out of the smoke and many of them stick to falling water droplets. Some of the water that is sprayed into the smoke turns to steam and travels up the chimney. Have you ever seen the chimney of an incinerator with its huge greyish white plume? Many people believe this is smoke, but it is actually the mist created as this steam turns back into water.

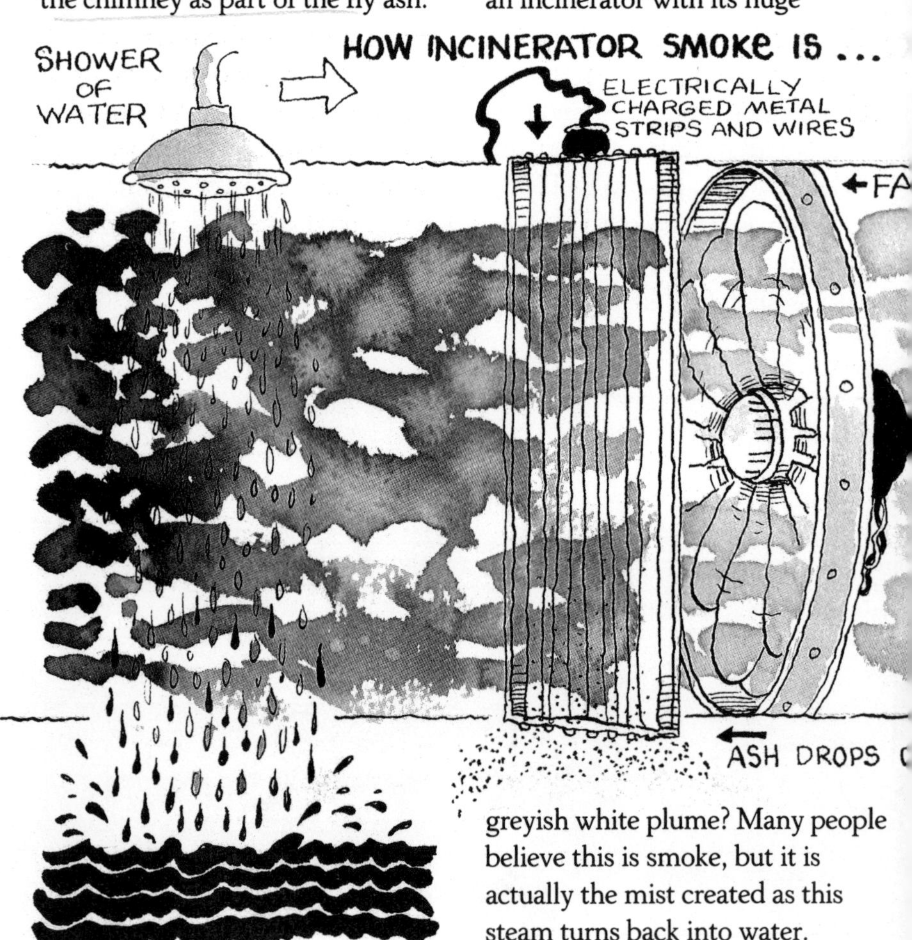

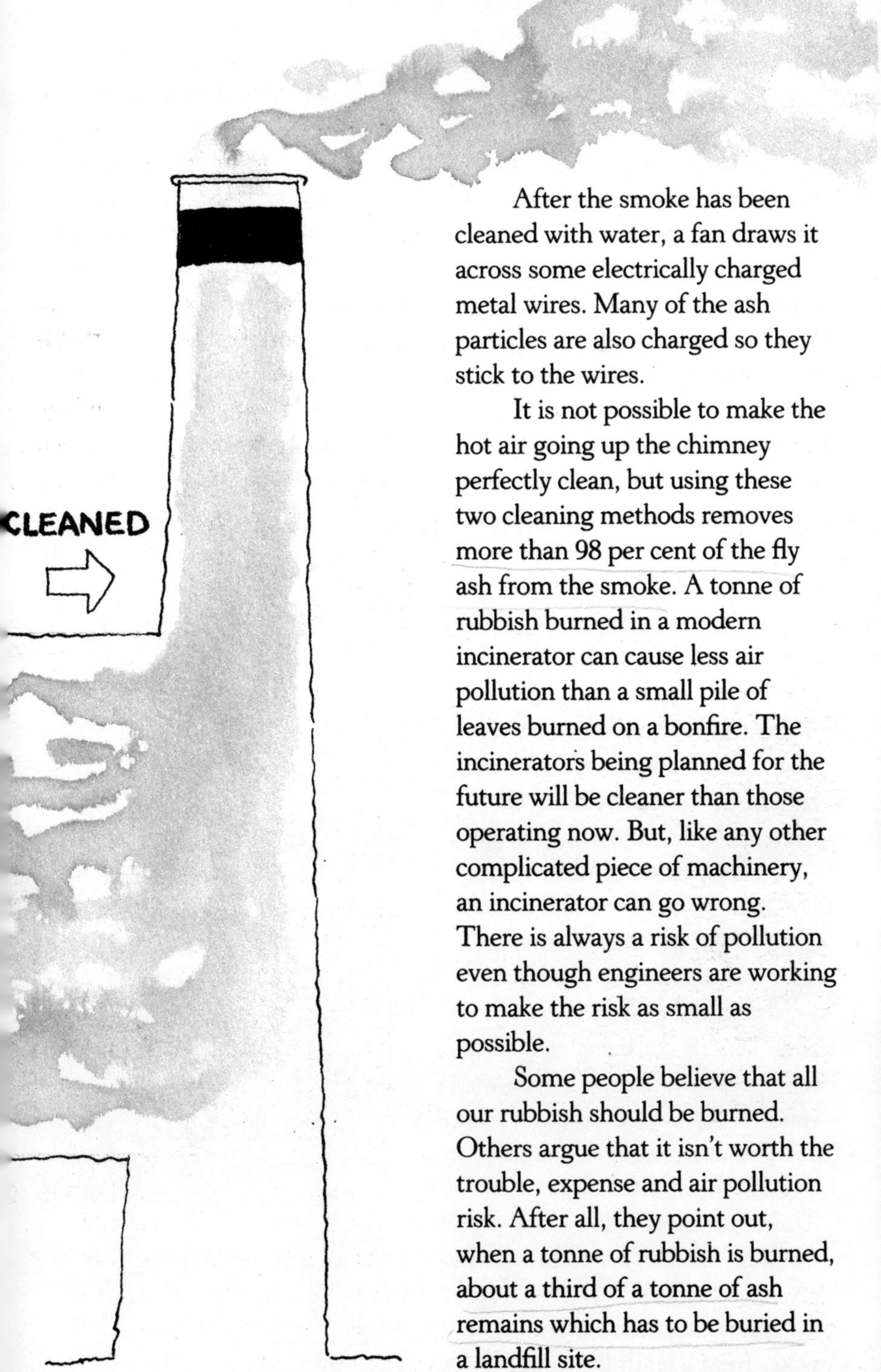

After the smoke has been cleaned with water, a fan draws it across some electrically charged metal wires. Many of the ash particles are also charged so they stick to the wires.

It is not possible to make the hot air going up the chimney perfectly clean, but using these two cleaning methods removes more than 98 per cent of the fly ash from the smoke. A tonne of rubbish burned in a modern incinerator can cause less air pollution than a small pile of leaves burned on a bonfire. The incinerators being planned for the future will be cleaner than those operating now. But, like any other complicated piece of machinery, an incinerator can go wrong. There is always a risk of pollution even though engineers are working to make the risk as small as possible.

Some people believe that all our rubbish should be burned. Others argue that it isn't worth the trouble, expense and air pollution risk. After all, they point out, when a tonne of rubbish is burned, about a third of a tonne of ash remains which has to be buried in a landfill site.

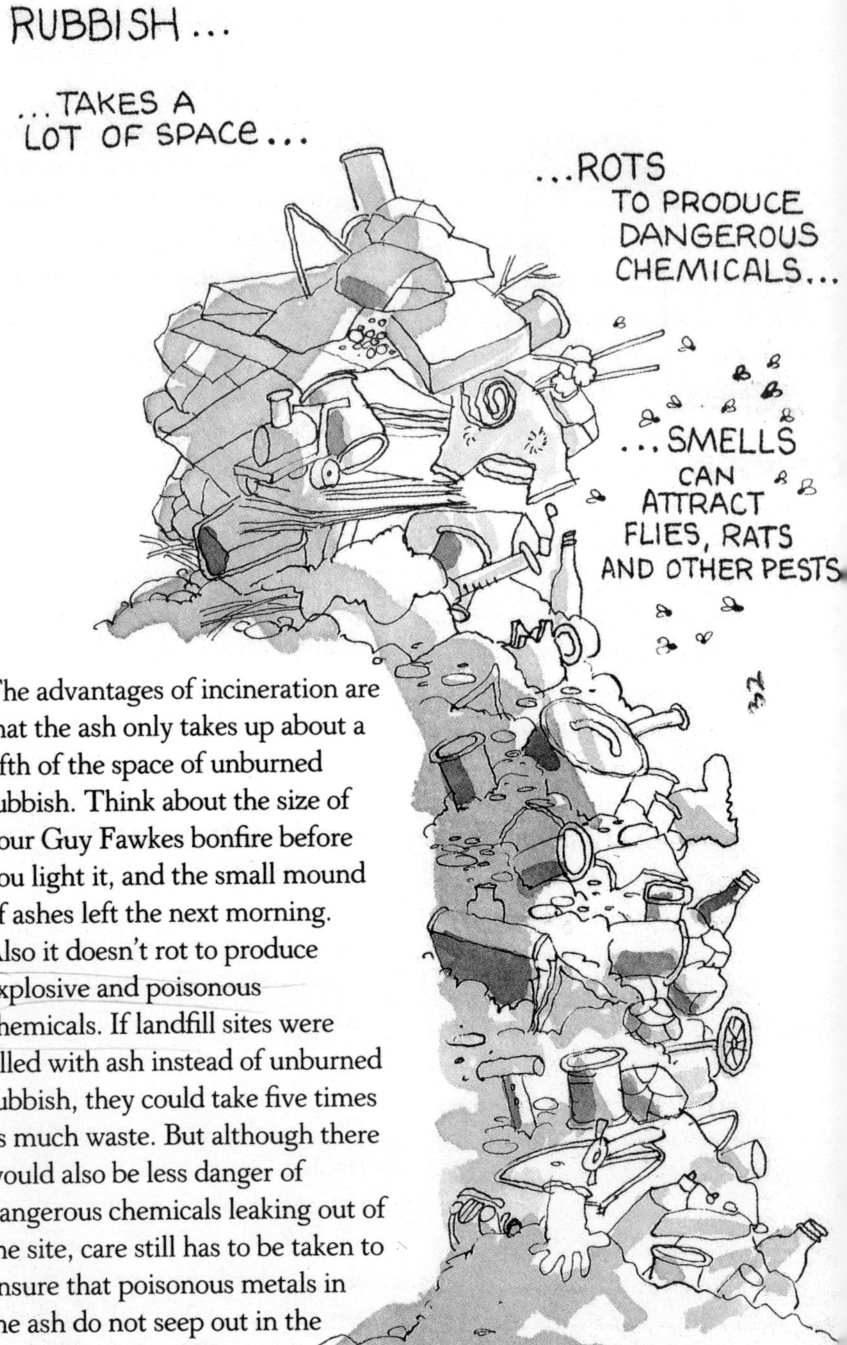

RUBBISH...

...TAKES A LOT OF SPACE...

...ROTS TO PRODUCE DANGEROUS CHEMICALS...

...SMELLS CAN ATTRACT FLIES, RATS AND OTHER PESTS

The advantages of incineration are that the ash only takes up about a fifth of the space of unburned rubbish. Think about the size of your Guy Fawkes bonfire before you light it, and the small mound of ashes left the next morning. Also it doesn't rot to produce explosive and poisonous chemicals. If landfill sites were filled with ash instead of unburned rubbish, they could take five times as much waste. But although there would also be less danger of dangerous chemicals leaking out of the site, care still has to be taken to ensure that poisonous metals in the ash do not seep out in the water from a landfill site.

Another advantage of incineration is that it allows us to make some use of rubbish. Much of the waste we throw away contains a great deal of energy. Burning it creates heat to warm water or generate electricity. After the burning is complete most of the metal from the rubbish is left behind in the ash. By drawing a large magnet over the ash, the iron and steel can be collected and re-used.

One big disadvantage of burning rubbish is the cost. The equipment needed to make incinerators run cleanly and safely is very expensive and burning a tonne of rubbish in an incinerator can cost more than three times as much as burying it directly in a landfill site.

So neither the burning nor the landfill solutions are ideal. Both are costly, and finding better methods of waste disposal could cost even more. Should we worry about costs when our environment is threatened? Or should we be looking for new and different solutions?

... BURNING RUBBISH ...

CAN PROVIDE USEFUL ENERGY ...

ASH DOESN'T ROT, ... SMELL OR ATTRACT FLIES

ASH TAKES UP LESS SPACE ...

..AND.. USEFUL METALS CAN BE MORE EASILY RECLAIMED ...

... BUT ...

...THERE'S ALWAYS THE RISK OF AIR POLLUTION ...

AND REDUCING THE RISK IS EXPENSIVE

Getting to Know Your Rubbish

No matter how good we become at disposing of other people's rubbish, it will never be cheap or easy to do. And there will always be the risk of pollution. If the rubbish mountain continues to grow, the problems will grow too.

The obvious answer is to make less rubbish. It seems perfectly simple, but none of the solutions to the rubbish problem is simple.

The best way to get ideas is to have a closer look at the problem. You could tip out your dustbin at the end of the week and have a good poke around. But that would not only make you extremely unpopular with your parents, teachers and friends (rubbish can be very smelly), it would also be very dangerous. Apart from broken glass and sharp metal, there would be the danger of bacteria and poisonous chemicals. Instead, keep a chart near your dustbin and make a note of everything that goes into the bin. What is it made of? Could it be re-used? Could it be recycled? Is it dangerous? What is the best way of disposing of it?

Do We Need So Many Throwaways?

One way to reduce the amount of rubbish we have to throw out of our homes would be to reduce the amount of rubbish we bring into our homes. As you think about the rubbish in your bin, ask yourself how the various items got there. How many of them were made to be thrown away as soon as their job was done?

Are there things in your rubbish bin that were thrown away just because they are dirty? Cloth handkerchieves can be washed and used again and again, but nowadays many people use paper tissues and throw them away after one or two noseblows. Paper towels, napkins and baby's nappies are also widely used instead of cloth.

Most 'fast food' restaurants use disposable cups, plates and cutlery so they don't have to wash up after their customers. This saves them time, which costs money. But it also creates unnecessary rubbish and highlights a further problem – litter. Because so many people believe rubbish is someone else's problem, they simply throw down rubbish on the street. Look at the main shopping street in your town at the end of a Saturday. Is it strewn with litter? Would it look better and be cleaner and safer if it were tidy. Are we all responsible for keeping it that way?

A lot of the things we read are disposable too. Not many people are interested in last week's newspapers so they just get thrown away, and the only home for last month's magazines is the dentist's waiting room. Most people write with disposable pens which can't be refilled so they're tossed in the bin. Think about all the writing and drawing paper you use and throw away. When your grandparents were in school, almost all children used slates which could be wiped clean and used again.

Some people complain that a lot of the rubbish they throw away is stuff they didn't want in the first place. 'Special offers', requests for money and free newspapers get shoved through people's letterboxes. Most people don't know why this 'junk mail' is being sent to them. And they don't know how to stop it being sent.

Another group of throwaways that many people complain about is packaging. It seems as though every time we go shopping, we bring home a bin load of bags, boxes, pots, jars, cans, tubes, bottles and wrapping. Is it all necessary?

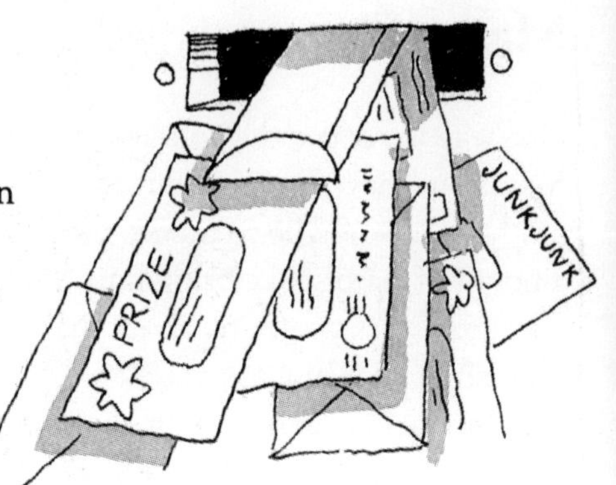

Packaging Pros and Cons

Some people believe that shops and manufacturers should work to reduce the amount of packaging that surround the things we buy. Everything we buy in a supermarket now comes in a package; even fruit is put in a plastic bag. And some packaging seems to be far more elaborate than it needs to be. When you go shopping, look carefully how goods are packaged. How much of it is for show? How much is essential and for what reasons? Why are there several layers on some packages? Choose a product which you feel is overpackaged and design an effective and attractive package using the minimum materials.

Shopkeepers point out that, while there may be some extra decoration on items like chocolates and perfume which are sold as gifts, most packaging is absolutely necessary. People like shopping in supermarkets because they can see everything that is for sale, pick things up and put them back if they decide not to buy them. This wouldn't be safe if things weren't wrapped. Apart from the dangers of food accidentally getting dirty, there have been cases of people deliberately putting poison and dangerous objects like pieces of glass into items that are on display in shops. Extra packaging is often needed to help protect people from this sort of tampering.

There is usually a reason for packaging but it may be hard to see at first. For example, toothpaste comes in a tube, so why is it sold inside a box as well? The answer is that the square box makes it easier to pack the tubes for the trip from the factory to the shop. It also makes it easier to stack the toothpaste on the shelves and prevents them from being accidentally squeezed before they're bought.

Food manufacturers point out that many of the things we eat today simply wouldn't be possible without containers such as cans and jars to preserve them or wrappings to protect and contain them. How could we buy frozen peas if they weren't in a plastic bag?

Buying modern packaged food can actually reduce the amount of rubbish in your bin. When you buy instant mashed potatoes or oven-ready chips, for example, you may have a package to throw away but you don't have a binful of potato peelings. Unless you have a compost heap, these usually go to waste. If those peelings were just thrown in the food factory's bin, it would make no difference. But food manufacturers can often find uses for their waste which are not available to the householder. Starch can be extracted from the potato peel. Orange peel can be made into marmalade or squash. Similarly, buying a chicken in a plastic bag from a butcher's shop or supermarket saves a great deal of waste. It's true that you have to throw out the plastic bag, but if you had bought the chicken as it comes from the farm, its head, feet and feathers would end up in your bin. The food manufacturer can use the head and feet to make gelatin and chicken stock. And the feathers can be washed, baled up and sold to the manufacturers of duvets and feather pillows.

How many bottles, cartons and jars are in your bin? Liquids like drinks and shampoos have to come in containers, of course, but do they have to be throwaway containers? In areas where milk is delivered door to door, the empty milk bottles are washed and re-filled at the dairy. Why do you think we do not use this system for other products? Would it be better to take the bottles back to the shop to refill them from a large container, or return them to the factory to be refilled and sold again.

Shopkeepers and manufacturers say that selling things in brand new containers is more convenient for everyone and it makes it easier to ensure the quality and safety of the product. They believe their customers prefer it.

Also transporting loads of empty bottles back to the factory would mean burning fuel and making air pollution. Re-using milk bottles is economical because the empty bottles are returned to the dairy on the same journey as the full ones are collected for delivery. Re-using other containers would only be economical if all the liquids we buy came in identical containers that were strong enough to be thoroughly cleaned, sterilized and re-used many times.

Nowadays, the liquids we buy come in a wide variety of bottles from many different factories. Even if all the shop's customers were willing to bring in their empty bottles, packing them up and hiring lorries and drivers to deliver them back to all the factories would make re-using the bottles cost much much more than burning them in the most expensive incinerator. It could even cause more pollution.

There may be a reason for all the different sorts of packaging we bring home and throw away, but it is up to us to decide if it is a good reason. Each of us makes this decision many times when we shop. For example, if we decide to buy a large bag containing lots of small packets of crisps, we will take home more rubbish than we would if we bought one big bag of crisps. Crisps in small packets cost more too. But many people choose to buy them because they're more convenient. In fact, since crisps begin to go stale once the bag is open, buying the smaller packets could lead to less food being wasted.

More and more food is being sold in packets that hold just one serving – yoghurts, juice, even cooked meals. These 'individual serving' packets mean a lot more rubbish going in the bin. The cooked meals often come in a box with a plastic inner wrapper and a 'microwave-able' plastic dish with a lid. Does your family buy food in individual serving packets? Do you think the extra convenience worth the extra rubbish? What do the other members of your family think?

There are probably lots of things in your bin that don't need to be there and perhaps they won't be there in the future if people in your family think about the rubbish problem when they shop. But a lot of the throwaways in our bins are essential to the sort of life we lead today. To stop using them would mean making big changes to the way we live – bigger changes than most people would want to make.

Luckily, there is another way to make less rubbish. Instead of just sending it off to an incinerator or landfill site, we could find ways of using the stuff we don't want.

Making Use of Rubbish

As you look at the list of rubbish in your bin ask yourself if any of it shouldn't really be there because a use could be found for it.

Perhaps some of the paper could be bundled together and used as a notepad. Empty jars could be used to store things, such as buttons, screws or pencils. If you like gardening, you could use things like yoghurt pots as containers for starting seedlings. Many gardeners use kitchen waste to make compost to fertilize and improve the soil of the garden.

Why don't you try making compost? Waste is turned into compost by Nature's recycling bacteria so to make compost you have to become a bacteria farmer and build a heap of waste that is an ideal place for compost-making bacteria to live. Cut the top and bottom off a cardboard box and then cut several 3 cm slits in each of the four walls to allow air to get into the heap. Place the box over an area of soil so that earthworms can burrow up into the compost and help the bacteria digest the waste. You can put in fruit and vegetable waste, grass clippings, and dead leaves. Add some manure to the heap if you can get some. If not, the litter and

droppings from a rabbit or guinea pig work nearly as well. Make sure the waste is well mixed.

The heap must be moist, but not wet, so cover it to keep out heavy rain. Sprinkle on water regularly. The compost heap will get quite warm inside and, after a year, the waste will have turned into a brownish black, crumbly material. If it doesn't look like this and if it is very smelly, the wrong bacteria have probably been at work and it's best not to put it on the garden.

This is a start, but most of our rubbish cannot be used again as it is. So we must begin to look at other ways of using it. And to find uses for rubbish on a scale large enough to make a real difference to the size of the rubbish mountain, we must all work together. And we must use organization and technology.

The most promising approach is to look at the materials rubbish is made of and think of ways they could be re-used. Over 95 per cent of household rubbish is made up of materials that fall into these seven classes:

– glass
– metal
– textiles (rags and old clothes)
– plastic
– paper and cardboard
– food waste
– fines (tiny particles of dust and ashes).

The rubbish from homes all over the world is made of these same classes of materials, but the proportions in each class can be very different in different areas. This means that the best ways of using rubbish are likely to be

different in different parts of the world.

In the poorest areas of the world, rubbish is largely made up of waste from the **preparation** of food. Bins from the wealthier areas contain more wasted food and a great deal of glass, metal, paper, cardboard and plastic from the packaging of consumer goods and prepared foods. American and Canadian 'garbage cans' usually contain more paper and cardboard than European rubbish bins. Large numbers of trees are grown in North America, so paper, which is made from trees, is especially cheap and easy to throw away.

If you try to separate the rubbish in your bin into the seven classes you will soon find out one of the big problems with using the materials from rubbish. Many of the materials may be useful, but once they are all mixed together in a bin, getting at them individually is very difficult, or even impossible. Some packages, for example, are made of several different types of materials firmly stuck together.

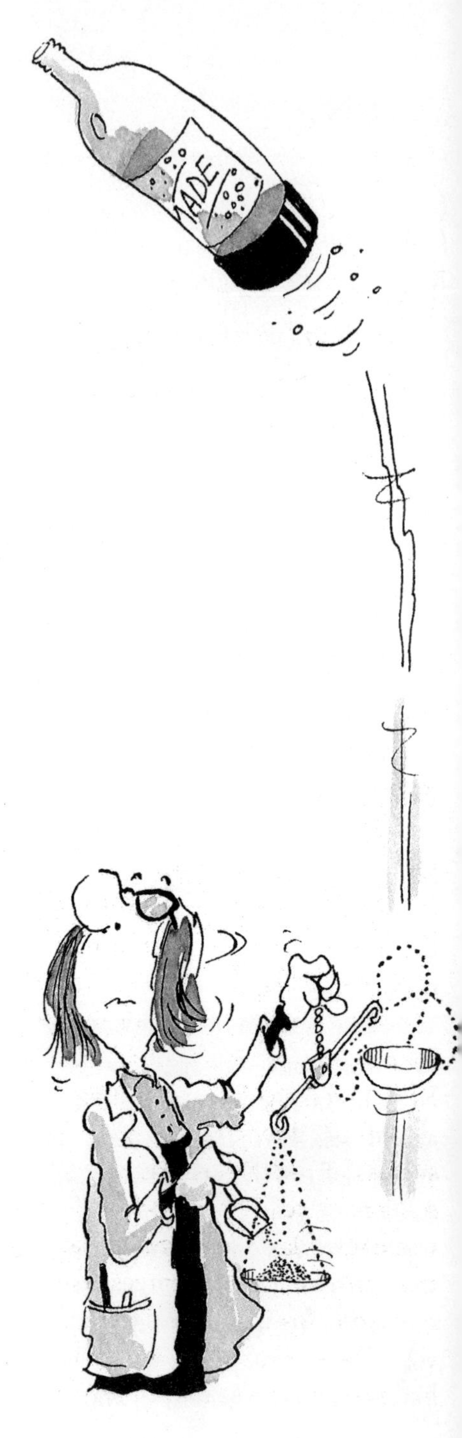

Write to your local council and ask how much rubbish they have to deal with and what proportion of it falls into each of the seven classes. They will have analysed and classified samples.

The information may contain some surprises. The proportions are worked out by weight so plastic, which can take up so much space in bins, usually makes up less than 5 per cent of the weight of household rubbish. In areas where a lot of people heat their homes by open fires, the rubbish contains a lot of fines and very little paper. This is because a lot of their waste paper is burned on the fire. In cities, where very few people have fires, paper can make up over 30 per cent of the rubbish.

See if you can find out how much of the waste made in your area is put to use. Are any useful materials separated from your rubbish after it is collected? Do people in your area keep some useful materials separate from the rest of your rubbish? Which of the materials are used and what are they used for?

Using Waste Materials

Many people believe that we should recycle our waste by using the materials from our rubbish to make new things.

This sounds like an ideal solution to the rubbish problem. Recycling is the waste-handling system which Nature has used successfully for thousands of millions of years. And re-using waste materials would mean that the Earth's natural resources, like metal ore, fossil fuels and trees, would be used more slowly. But like everything else to do with rubbish, recycling is a lot more complicated than it seems.

For a material to be recycled, it has to be separated from the rest of the rubbish. Machinery is needed to change the old material into a form that can be used to make new things. And the new things made from the recycled material have to be worthwhile. People must be willing to pay money to cover at least some of the cost of recycling.

Most of our waste materials could be used in some way, but each material has to be treated quite differently.

Glass

Glass is the easiest material to recycle. It isn't difficult to recognise glass objects and keep them separate from the rest of the rubbish. The glass has to be separated into different colours, but this isn't difficult either. And there is no shortage of factories to reclaim glass. Once the dirt, labels, and things like bottle tops have been removed and the old glass has been melted, it is just as good as glass newly made from purified sand. And the reclaimed glass is quite a bit cheaper too.

Metal

It might seem as though metal should be as easy to recycle as glass since it can also be melted down and used to make new objects. But there are added problems. It isn't so easy to separate different kinds of waste metals and some throwaway items, tin cans for example, are made of a mixture of metals. Scrap metal must sometimes be transported hundreds of kilometres to a factory where it can be reclaimed. All this can make reclaiming metal quite expensive. Even so, it is almost always practical to recycle waste metal, especially if large loads can be collected together.

Textiles

Cloth is made from tiny strands or 'fibres'. These are spun into thicker strands and then woven or knitted to make fabric. The fibres from old clothes can be reworked to make new cloth but these fibres have been dyed and then worn and washed many times. It is usually impossible to turn them into high quality cloth again, but they can be used to make things like stuffing for furniture. And fibres of cotton and linen are used to make paper. The best way to recycle old clothes is to hand them on to someone else, give them to a charity shop or, if they are really worn, to use them as rags or dusters, rather than buy new, disposable ones.

Plastic

Old plastic can be melted down to make new plastic objects, but here the practical problems are much more serious. Most of the plastic we throw in the bin is made up of six basic types. Although most people would have trouble telling them apart, each kind of plastic is quite different. For recycling to work, the different plastics have to be separated perfectly because if one sort of plastic were melted down with another, the mixture could not be re-used. Some manufacturers have begun labelling the plastic containers they make with the name of the plastic so that people will be able to separate the different sorts more easily. Meanwhile, to help stop durable plastic litter building up, scientists have been looking at the possibility of making things of plastics that can be broken down either by sunlight or by organisms. But it is obviously very difficult to invent plastics that are durable as long as they are useful, and easily broken down when they're no longer needed.

The main reason it isn't practical at the moment to recycle plastics is that plastic is very easy to make from oil. Oil is a vital natural resource but, for the time being at least, it seems so plentiful that many people believe that it isn't worth going to all the trouble of recycling plastic.

But there is another way of using waste plastic that would be practical and it would save oil too. The plastic could be used as fuel. A mixture of plastic and waste paper formed into lumps could be burned like coal in furnaces designed to ensure that poisonous gases don't escape.

Paper and cardboard

Paper and cardboard are made of the tiny fibres of plants, usually trees, which are pressed together to make a flat sheet. To recycle paper the fibres have to be separated again, washed, sometimes bleached, then pressed together again to make new paper.

Why not try recycling paper yourself? Simply soak scraps of old paper in warm water for about ten minutes then beat them with a whisk until the water is mushy and full of paper fibres. Slide a fine wire mesh into the water and lift it up through the paper pulp so that a thin layer of paper fibres is caught in the mesh. Allow the water to drip off, then carefully place it fibre side down on a piece of blotting paper. Lift up the mesh so that the fibres are left behind and put a second sheet of blotting paper on top. Press the sheets with a rolling pin and then iron until they are dry. Peel back the blotting paper and find your sheet of recycled paper in the middle.

Recycling paper is now becoming more practical, but in the past people who wanted to make and sell recycled paper had a lot of trouble finding anyone who wanted to buy it. This lead to some embarrassing problems. People who had carefully saved stacks and stacks of paper for recycling were horrified to discover that the collectors just disposed of it along with the rest of their rubbish because they couldn't find anyone to recycle it.

Since then, the technology for making new paper out of old has improved and many more paper-reclaiming factories have been built. Today, newspapers, toilet paper, paper towels and many other products contain at least some recycled paper, and the range of quality recycled paper products is steadily increasing. Recycled paper is not necessarily cheaper than new paper but many people now want to buy it in order to help save natural resources and make less rubbish. This is a first step towards a new and more responsible attitude to waste.

Paper recycling works best if the people who are saving their waste paper separate it into different 'grades'. Each grade can only be recycled to make more paper of that grade. Most newspapers contain lots of recycled fibres because saving old newspapers is easy. Higher grades of paper are less likely to be recycled because they are used for things that are not meant to be thrown away – this book for example.

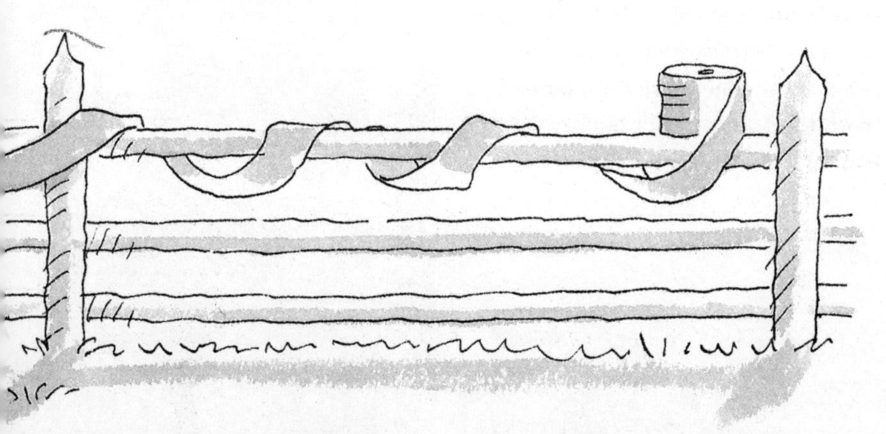

Food waste

Our food waste can be eaten by many other living creatures and they are the first link of the natural recycling chain which ends with nutrients from the waste being released into the soil to make it more fertile. If our food waste was kept in conditions that would encourage recycling micro-organisms to grow quickly, in a very short time it could become compost to fertilize gardens and farmland.

Many people believe it will become practical to handle our food waste in this way, but scientists and engineers are still developing the technology to make it reliable and economical on a large scale. The compost made from food waste can't be too expensive or farmers and gardeners won't buy it. And great care has to be taken to make sure

that other sorts of rubbish aren't mixed in with the food waste that is being composted. This rubbish could damage soil and if it contained heavy metals, it would make any food grown on the compost unsafe to eat.

Nature has another way of handling waste that could also be useful. The bacteria which rot food waste in airless conditions, such as those found deep in a landfill, make gas as a waste product. If food waste were kept in conditions that encouraged these organisms to grow, they could turn it into useful fuel gas. But again, the technology to make this practical is still being developed.

Fines

Dust and ashes are the least useful of all the materials we throw away but since they don't rot or take up much space they are also the least difficult to dispose of.

Can We Lighten the Rubbish Load?

Finding ways to re-use the materials we now throw away really could shrink our rubbish mountain to a more manageable size. The problem is, none of the ideas for using waste can be made to work well unless there are some big changes to the ways we handle waste and the ways we make new things.

The changes have to begin at home. Most of us just toss most of our waste into one bin. Doing this turns useful materials into a load of rubbish. Almost every idea for using rubbish depends upon rubbish being sorted into its different materials. Machines that can separate the different kinds of waste are being developed, but it would be impossible for a machine to separate rubbish well enough to make best use of the materials it contains. It would be far better if we rubbish makers didn't let our different wastes get mixed up in the first place.

If everyone got into the habit of throwing their waste materials into different bins, a great deal less rubbish would have to be carted to the incinerators and landfill sites. Many communities already have programmes for recycling glass, metal and waste paper. Sometimes waste for recycling has to be delivered to a central collection point such as a 'bottle bank', and in some areas, material such as waste paper is regularly collected from the home.

But how many of the people in your neighbourhood separate their rubbish for recycling? You could do a survey to find out. Which waste materials do they save? Do they make compost? What reasons do people give for **not** working to recycle their waste?

Some of the people you survey might simply not know much about recycling or what to do with their waste materials. The authority responsible for collecting rubbish in your area could tell you about recycling programmes. And you could learn more by writing to the organizations involved in reclaiming waste and the environmental organizations that encourage recycling. (Their addresses are on page 62). Why not write an information sheet on recycling in your community and give a copy of it to people you survey who would like to know more about it? Try to use recycled paper for your information sheet and remember to write on both sides. Don't add to the rubbish problem.

Many people in your neighbourhood might be willing to separate their waste materials for recycling if there were regular collections of separated waste. If that is the case, talk to your local authority about starting up collections. In many areas, local charities collect this waste. The charity helps the community by reducing rubbish and they make money for the charity by selling the waste to factories which can reclaim and use the materials.

If people aren't willing to separate their rubbish for recycling, could they be persuaded to change their minds? In some countries, people lose money if they throw away drink containers. When they buy a drink, they have to pay a little extra money as a 'deposit' and they only get the money back when they return the empty bottle or can. The deposit idea is a good way of preventing littering because, if some people throw empty bottles or cans on the ground, other people in the neighbourhood will often pick them up, return them and collect the deposit money.

Another way of using money to encourage people to stop making so much rubbish is to charge them each time their rubbish is taken away. The more waste they put in the bin, the more they would have to pay. The more useful waste they separated out for recycling the less they would have to pay.

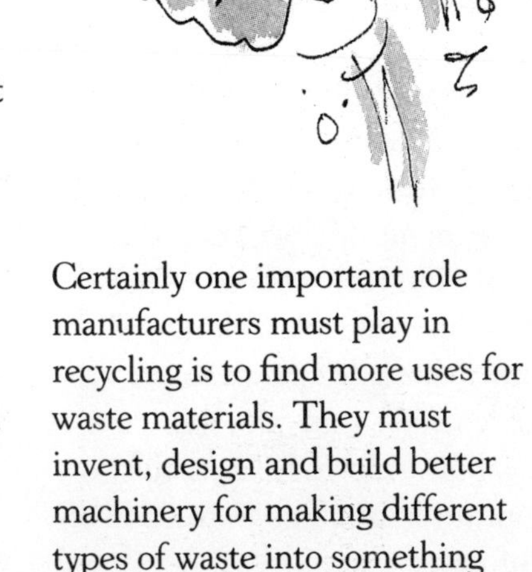

But even if everyone was willing to work hard to see that their waste is recycled, some of the throwaway items we bring home couldn't be re-used because they are made of a mixture of two or more different materials. This isn't always a problem because the different materials can often be separated. For example, the paper labels on glass bottles and jars come off easily. But some of the throwaway drink cartons we buy are made of layers of plastic, metal foil and more plastic that are impossible to separate.

Manufacturers must also make some changes if we are to succeed in recycling more of our waste. Some people believe that factories should stop making packages of mixed material and that glass containers, which are easy to recycle, should be used more often instead of plastic.

Certainly one important role manufacturers must play in recycling is to find more uses for waste materials. They must invent, design and build better machinery for making different types of waste into something useful.

But the final step in putting rubbish to use has again to be made by us, the rubbish makers. We have to be ready to sort and dispose of our rubbish so that as much as possible can be recycled, and to buy recycled products.

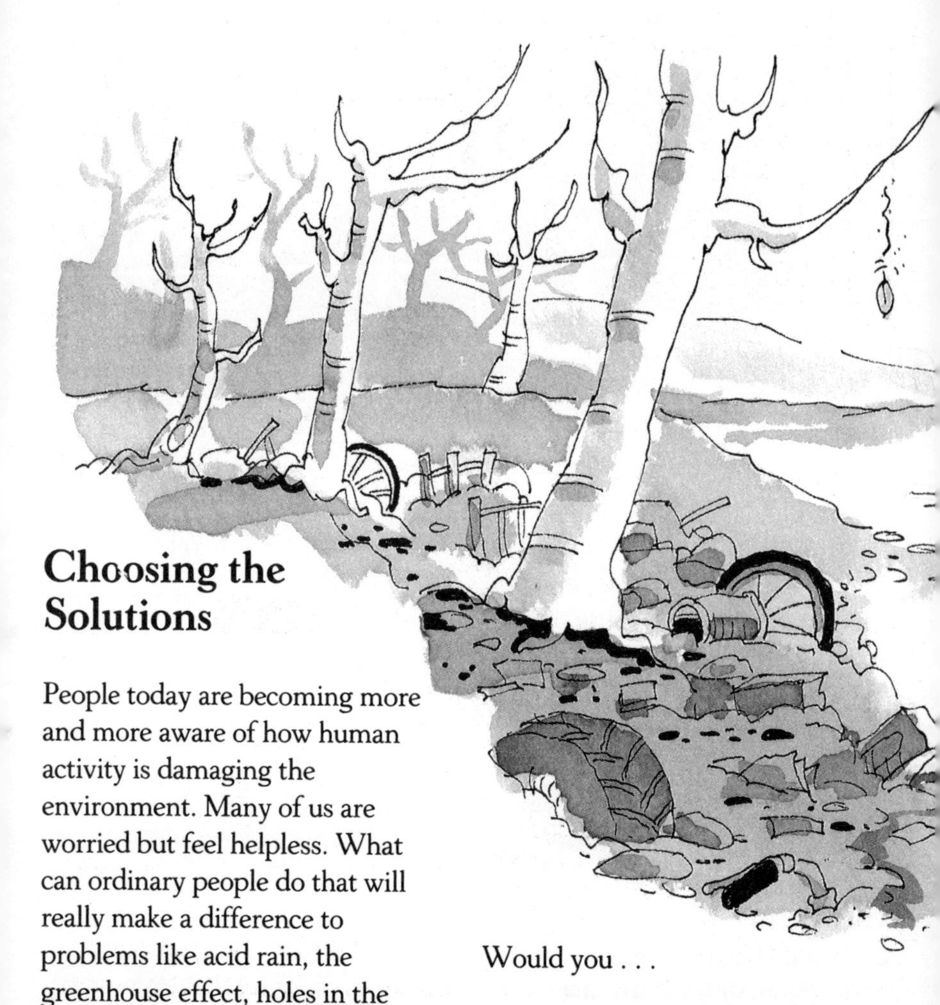

Choosing the Solutions

People today are becoming more and more aware of how human activity is damaging the environment. Many of us are worried but feel helpless. What can ordinary people do that will really make a difference to problems like acid rain, the greenhouse effect, holes in the ozone layer, and the destruction of rainforests?

Rubbish is something we can do something about. In fact, rubbish pollution can only be prevented if we – the rubbish makers – are willing to help. What changes would you and your family be willing to make to help solve the rubbish problem?

Would you . . .

. . . write to all the people who send you unwanted paper and tell them to stop?

. . . make changes in the things you buy and the food you eat so that you don't use so many throwaway items?

. . . carefully separate your waste so that the different materials can be used?

. . . buy products made of reclaimed waste and materials that are easy to recycle?
. . . live next to a landfill site if disposal engineers decide that your neighbourhood would be a safe place to bury rubbish?
. . . join an environmental group and help them to increase awareness of the problems, and put pressure on those who can make changes?

Rubbish is not a problem which will go away. If we continue without making changes, it will simply become worse and worse. It is up to the rubbish makers – you and me – to understand that our rubbish is not simply someone else's problem once we throw it in the bin. We must all act, individually and together, to find better ways of disposing of our loads of rubbish.

Useful Addresses

United Kingdom Reclamation Council
16 High Street
Brampton, Huntingdon
Cambs. PE18 8TU

British Waste Paper Association
Alexander House Business Centre
Station Road
Aldershot
Hants. GU11 1BQ

British Paper and Board Industries Federation
Papermakers House
Rivenhall Road
Westlea, Swindon
Wilts. SN5 7BE

British Glass Manufacturers Federation
Northumberland Road
Sheffield S10 2UA

British Plastics Federation
5 Belgrave Square
London SW1X 8PH

World Action for Recycling Energy and Materials from Rubbish (W.A.R.M.E.R.)
83 Mount Ephraim
Royal Tunbridge Wells
Kent TN4 8BS

Friends of the Earth
26–28 Underwood Street
London N1 7JQ

Greenpeace
30–31 Islington Green
London N1 8XE

Glossary

aerobic using oxygen

bacteria microscopic single-cell creature

biodegradable capable of being broken down by living creatures, especially bacteria

disposable designed to be thrown away after one use

environment surroundings

fly ash tiny particles in smoke from incinerators

fossil plant or animal remains preserved in the earth

fossil fuel fuel such as coal and oil formed from decayed plants or animals

hunter-gatherer someone who finds their food by hunting wild animals and collecting wild plants

incinerator furnace designed for burning rubbish

landfill sites areas used for dumping and compacting rubbish

leachate liquid containing dangerous chemicals which can seep out of landfill sites

micro-organism living thing too small to be seen with the naked eye

midden hole in which to throw rubbish

nomadic with no permanent home, wandering from place to place

nutrient substance which living things need to consume

ore natural mineral from which metals or other substances can be extracted

organism living thing

pollute contaminate, make dirty

recycle change waste to a re-usable material

synthetic new chemicals made by humans, usually from fossil fuels